NED KELLY

and the

Green Sash

STORY BY MARK GREENWOOD
ILLUSTRATIONS BY FRANÉ LESSAC

WALKER BOOKS
AND SUBSIDIARIES

LONDON • BOSTON • SYDNEY • AUCKLAND

I do not pretend that I have led a blameless life, or that one fault justified another, but the public, judging a case like mine, should remember that the darkest life may have a bright side, and after the worst has been said against a man, he may, if he is heard, tell a story in his own rough way ...

Condemned Cell, Melbourne Gaol, November 1880

I was raised on the banks of a winter creek. Home was a ramshackle hut with a bark roof and dirt floor. My family kept cows on a rented farm and battled to scrape a living. To earn a few shillings we sold milk and butter on the overland track, where coaches carted gold from the diggings.

My father was a convict who could ill afford another brush with the law and my uncles and cousins were no strangers to crime. I soon learned the tricks of their trade – a chook here, a pig there, a chestnut mare hidden among the river gums until a reward was offered.

The traps said we were Irish riffraff, drawn to trouble like maggots to a summer's day. Those big-bellied unicorns showed no pity for our misfortune. If you knew how we suffered, you would say our clan could not be blamed for stealing from wealthy squatters.

Each day I took a short cut to school following the crooked path of Hughes Creek. After soaking rain the track was so rotten it could bog a duck, but I always arrived before the bell to avoid the leather strap.

One morning I spied a classmate balanced on a branch that spanned the creek. Richard Shelton was fishing for his hat with a stick.

I hollered out but he slipped and vanished in the rapids.

I made a sign of the cross and waded into water so icy cold it stole my breath. Kicking and splashing, fighting the power of the flood, I swam out to the drowning boy and dragged him free from a tangle of snags.

The current swept us downstream to an elbow in the creek. I snatched a branch and wrenched Richard Shelton into the bulrushes. He coughed up muck when I squeezed his chest, and then he bawled for his mother.

Mrs Shelton made a mighty fuss when she recognised the limp form clinging to my back. She ushered us inside the Royal Mail Hotel.

I soaked in a steaming tub until my skin wrinkled. When I was dry Mrs Shelton seated me beside a crackling fire.

"You're an angel," she whispered.

Instead of damper and dripping, I feasted on tasty pork steaks and fried eggs.

That evening a buggy pulled up outside our hut. It was Mr Shelton.

"You're a plucky lad for saving my son," he said.

I was rewarded with a hero's sash. It was made of green silk with gold bullion fringes that glinted in the firelight.

"Wear it with pride," he said, "as an emblem of your courage."

Ma said it was the grandest sash she'd ever seen.

I was the proudest boy the sun ever shone on when Father tied it
around my waist. "It's shamrock-green," he said, "the colour of Ireland."

I turned twelve the following summer when drought turned paddocks
to dust. Our misery was made worse when traps arrested Father for
duffing a stray calf. A cramped prison and a dose of dropsy drove him
to an early grave. Packed in a bullock wagon, we travelled north to be
closer to our clan.

At our new hut on Eleven Mile Creek, I received my first lessons in bushranging. Harry Power acquainted me with his hide-outs in the mountains and together we led a reckless life. The cunning old fox bailed up stagecoaches and robbed the rich while I steadied horses for a quick getaway.

The forces of the law plotted against me and I got used to the
pinch of iron shackles. After three years in the dungeons of Pentridge,
I returned home and split timber for fencing. But I was blamed for
stealing cattle and horses. Everyone looked upon me as if I were
a black snake.

Traps ransacked our home, upsetting dishes, breaking eggs, emptying flour from casks. Those fat-necked unicorns insulted my mother and frightened my sisters.

Such cruel conduct made my blood boil. I gave them fair warning – if they kept it up, I'd give 'em something to talk about.

The  Argus.

No: 10,096.   MELBOURNE, SATURDAY, OCTOBER 12, 1878.   PRICE 3d.

OUTLAWS OF THE WOMBAT RANGES

THE KELLYS ARE A MENACE to law-abiding citizens. Their squalid shanty is frequented by ruffians and horse thieves. When Constable Fitzpatrick paid a visit to enforce a warrant a violent brawl erupted. Mrs Kelly dented the trooper's helmet with a spade. Ned Kelly fired three shots, lodging a ball of lead in the trooper's wrist.

Mrs Kelly was sentenced to three years with hard labour. Ned Kelly offered to give himself up in exchange for his mother's freedom but his plea was ignored. A reward has been offered for his capture.

It is believed that the fugitive is hiding in the Wombat Ranges with his brother, Dan, and two larrikins, Steve Hart and Joe Byrne. Armed patrols continue to scour the gullies and gorges but their movements are telegraphed across the bush. So long as there are sympathisers willing to screen criminals from justice, the police are placed at great disadvantage.

MRS KELLY AT HER TRIAL IN BEECHWORTH

NED KELLY

DAN KELLY

JOE BYRNE

STEVE HART

The Ovens and Murray Advertiser,

BEECHWORTH, SATURDAY, OCTOBER 26, 1878.

MURDER OF POLICE

CONSTABLE McINTYRE HAS arrived with intelligence of a tragic encounter. Police, hunting for the notorious Ned Kelly, set up camp on the banks of Stringybark Creek. Sergeant Kennedy and Constable Scanlon were out on mounted patrol. Troopers Lonigan and McIntyre were preparing afternoon tea when bushrangers advanced from the spear grass and demanded they bail up. McIntyre threw up his hands but Lonigan reached for his revolver and received a fatal wound.

At twilight Sergeant Kennedy and Constable Scanlon rode into camp and a fierce gunfight erupted. Scanlon was mortally wounded. Sergeant Kennedy was last seen dodging bullets from tree to tree. There is every reason to fear the worst.

McIntyre escaped on a horse and made his way across rough country to bring news of the atrocious crime. A large number of police have been despatched. No effort will be spared to capture the bloodthirsty offenders.

GUNFIGHT AT STRINGYBARK CREEK

The Argus.

No. 10,135.   MELBOURNE, TUESDAY, DECEMBER 10, 1878.   PRICE 3d.

THE KELLY GANG AT EUROA

TOP RANKING OFFICERS head the hunt but the Kelly Gang continues to baffle police with false trails.

In broad daylight the wanted men descended on the town of Euroa. They ransacked a hawker's cart and fitted themselves out in whipcord trousers and fancy hats. They cut telegraph wires and robbed the bank of gold and silver.

The outlaws left town with an exhibition of trick riding. Ned Kelly leaned back in his saddle and boasted that the country would soon ring with his name. He hurdled a fence at full gallop and rode away triumphant.

The ruffians distributed the loot to their kin, displaying contempt for the law. The reward for their capture has been increased.

NED KELLY AND HIS GANG RIDING OUT OF EUROA

The Ovens and Murray Advertiser.

BEECHWORTH, MONDAY, FEBRUARY 10, 1879.

ANOTHER OUTRAGE BY THE KELLY GANG

THE KELLY GANG HAS RAIDED Jerilderie according to an eyewitness. Dressed in police jackets, the gang held up the bank and left town without a shot being fired.

The scoundrel, Ned Kelly, declared a school holiday in honour of their visit and dictated a rambling letter, demanding justice be done to his mother. He seeks no mercy for himself but threatens wicked mischief if his request is not complied with.

Police have been unable to discover the gang's hide-out but a special train carrying reinforcements is now travelling towards the district where the outlaws were last seen.

BAILING UP THE BANK AT JERILDERIE

POLICE DEPARTING ON THE HUNT FOR THE KELLY GANG

I do not wish to win a word of pity but I ask that my story be heard and considered. Let the hand of the law strike me down if it will. I don't care. My character could not be painted blacker but my conscience is clear. Circumstances forced us to become outlaws. We were desperate men, compelled to defend ourselves.

At a place only known to a few, we worked with hammer and fire. Helmets and breastplates, fashioned from ploughs, were shaped over logs stripped of bark. We traced charcoal bullseyes on trees and practised for battle with revolver and rifle.

Beyond the station at Glenrowan a length of rail was levered off the track. My intention was the speedy dispatch to kingdom come of a train full of wombat-headed, magpie-legged, splay-footed "officers of justice".

We bailed the townsfolk into a rickety inn. In the parlour we sang rebel songs and danced to the music of a concertina. I stared into the darkness and waited for the train to come rolling around the bend.

After midnight I allowed the schoolmaster to go home. I warned
him not to dream too loud but he betrayed my trust. Down the track,
he waved a candle behind a red scarf. I heard the squeal of locomotive
brakes. The train shuddered to a standstill. Traps crawled out of the
carriages like angry bull ants and quickly surrounded the inn.

We donned our suits of iron and stood side by side, rifles levelled to our shoulders.

"Fire away," I roared. "You can't hurt us."

The first volley of bullets riddled weatherboards and showered hostages with shards of glass.

A ball of lead ripped through my elbow. A second
passed from toe to heel. The rest of the gang retreated
into the darkened shanty. Faint from loss of blood, I limped across
a paddock behind the inn and passed the night on frosted ground.

I roused at daybreak and hobbled through the curling mist,
determined not to desert my mates. I rapped on my ironclad breast
with the butt of my revolver.

"Fire away, you snakes and toads," I cursed.

A barrage of lead sparked off my armour. I lurched from tree to tree,
returning fire with a pistol cradled over my shattered arm. The traps
aimed at my legs. I buckled with the force of each shotgun blast.

"I'm done," I cried and the weight of armour dragged me to my knees.

My eyes were swollen by bullets that had slammed into my helmet – my feet were numb, my hands peppered with lead. A doctor unbuckled the leather straps and forced apart two plates of iron.

I ran my bloody fingers through the silk sash wrapped around my waist. Once it was an emblem of courage – proof even my dark life had a bright side.

After the worst has been said against a man, he may, if he is heard, tell a story in his own rough way that may lead the public to soften their harsh thoughts about him.

I need no lead or powder to revenge my cause if words be louder.

Such is life.

The Kelly Gang

Edward Ned Kelly
(1855-1880)

Ned was the eldest son of Irish convict John "Red" Kelly and Ellen Quinn Kelly. Like his uncles and cousins, the Quinns and the Lloyds, Ned was frequently in and out of jail. He was an accomplished bushman, an expert rider, a sure shot with revolver or rifle and a champion boxer. Despite a petition with over 32,000 signatures calling for a reprieve, Ned Kelly was hanged on November 11th, 1880. His reputed last words were "Such is life".

↑ JERILDERIE

MURRAY RIVER

BROKEN RIVER

Kelly Country

EUROA

AVENEL

Steve Hart
(1859-1880)

Steve won fame as a jockey and for being the only person who could jump his horse over the railway gates at Wangaratta. He met Dan Kelly in Beechworth Gaol. Both were members of the "Greta Mob", a well-known gang of bush larrikins. According to legend, he was chopping wood when he threw down his axe and joined the Kellys, exclaiming, "Here's to a short life and a merry one!" Steve Hart perished in the inferno at Glenrowan Inn beside his mate, Dan Kelly.

BEVERIDGE

MELBOURNE
↓

Joe Byrne
(1857-1880)

Joe was a writer and a poet and could speak fluent Cantonese. He was also a first-class bushman and an expert marksman. With his revolver he rarely missed a two-shilling piece thrown in the air. Ned consulted him on strategy and said Joe "was as straight and true as steel". High-heeled boots were Joe Byrne's trademark.

NEW SOUTH WALES

WARBY RANGES

WANGARATTA

BEECHWORTH

GLENROWAN

OXLEY PLAINS

GRETA

BENALLA

STRINGYBARK CREEK

MANSFIELD

WOMBAT RANGES

VICTORIA

Dan Kelly
(1861-1880)

Dan was the youngest of the Kelly boys and the only member of the gang to be wounded at Stringybark Creek. He had his first run-in with the law at the age of ten. At seventeen he was wanted for horse stealing. By nineteen he was branded an outlaw. Despite the evidence of his charred remains being pulled from the ashes of the Glenrowan Inn, many people claim he escaped from the burning hotel.

The Green Sash

For over 100 years the whereabouts of Ned Kelly's most treasured possession was known only to a handful of people. The sash of honour was awarded to Ned by Esau Shelton of Avenel for rescuing his son from drowning.

The green sash was last worn beneath Ned's armour at the siege of Glenrowan. Doctor Nicholson dressed the outlaw's wounds after his capture and slipped the valuable memento into his bag on the morning of June 28th, 1880. Nothing was mentioned about Ned Kelly's sash in the doctor's statements and there was no reference to it in the press.

For many years the bloodstained relic was stored in England, along with other items of Doctor Nicholson's estate. The exact date the sash was returned to Australia is unknown. It is now displayed at the Benalla Costume and Pioneer Museum.

Ned Kelly's green sash is made of silk, backed with plain woollen fabric. It is 230 centimetres long, 14 centimetres wide and finished at each end with metallic gold fringing.

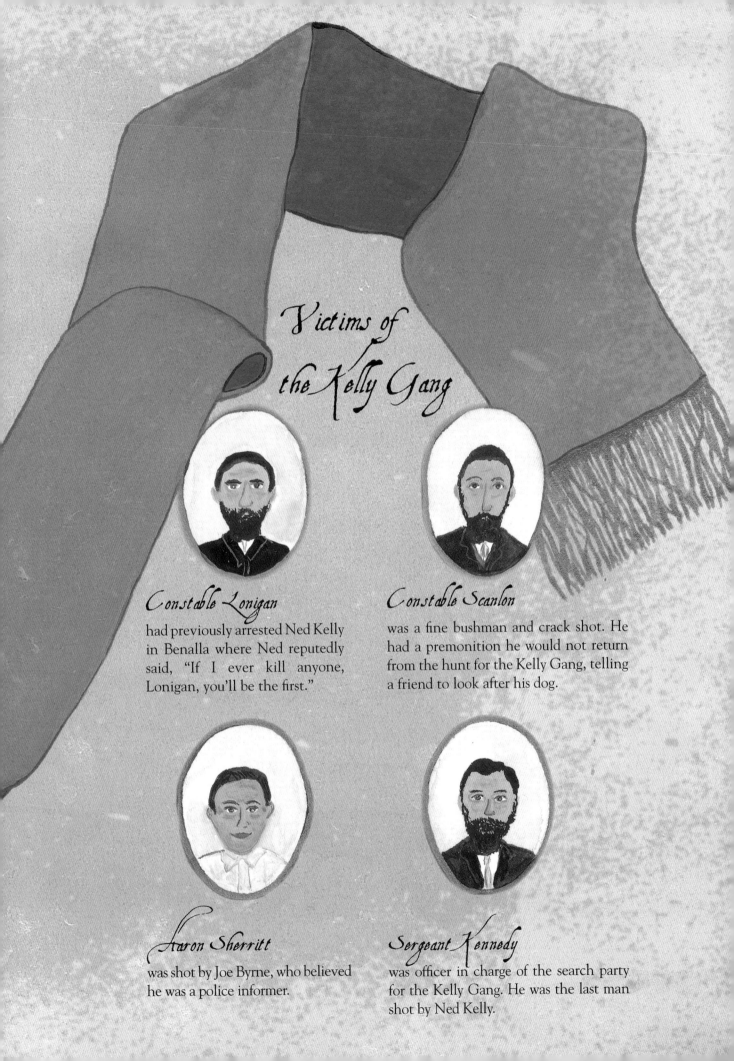

Victims of the Kelly Gang

Constable Lonigan

had previously arrested Ned Kelly in Benalla where Ned reputedly said, "If I ever kill anyone, Lonigan, you'll be the first."

Constable Scanlon

was a fine bushman and crack shot. He had a premonition he would not return from the hunt for the Kelly Gang, telling a friend to look after his dog.

Aaron Sherritt

was shot by Joe Byrne, who believed he was a police informer.

Sergeant Kennedy

was officer in charge of the search party for the Kelly Gang. He was the last man shot by Ned Kelly.

For Ned Kelly – for giving us a story to tell in our own rough way.

For Sergeant Kennedy, and Constables Lonigan and Scanlon, who lost their lives in the line of duty – we express our deepest sympathy to their descendants.

Special thanks to Robin Sadler from the Benalla & District Historical Society; staff at the Benalla Costume and Pioneer Museum; Nan and Tony O'Brien for the photos of Hughes Creek in flood; Brian McDonald at Australian History Promotions; Bob and Lesley Reece; Lyne and Frank Greenwood; Sarah Foster, Sue Whiting and Miriam Steenhauer.

SOURCES:

Blake, L, *Young Ned*, Neptune Press, Belmont, Victoria, 1980

Brown, M, *Ned Kelly, Australian Son*, Angus & Robertson, Sydney, 1981

Carey, P, *True History of the Kelly Gang*, University of Queensland Press, St Lucia, Queensland, 2000

Drew, R, *Our Sunshine*, Penguin Books, 1991

Jones, I, *Ned Kelly: A Short Life*, Lothian Books, Port Melbourne, Victoria, 1995

Kelly, E, *Babington letter* (July 1870), *Cameron letter* (December 1878), *Jerilderie letter* (February 1879), and various letters dictated in the Melbourne Gaol (1st-10th November, 1880)

McMenomy, K, *Ned Kelly, The Authentic Illustrated History*, Hardie Grant Books, South Yarra, Victoria, 2001

First published in 2010
by Walker Books Australia Pty Ltd
Locked Bag 22, Newtown
NSW 2042 Australia
www.walkerbooks.com.au

This edition published in 2014.

National Library of Australia Cataloguing-in-Publication entry:
Greenwood, Mark, author.
Ned Kelly and the green sash / Mark Greenwood; illustrations by Frané Lessac.
ISBN: 978 1 922244 59 8 (paperback)
Subjects: Kelly, Ned, 1855-1880.
         Bushrangers – Australia – Biography.
Other Authors/Contributors: Lessac, Frané, illustrator.
364.1552

Typeset in Goudy Old Style
Printed and bound in China